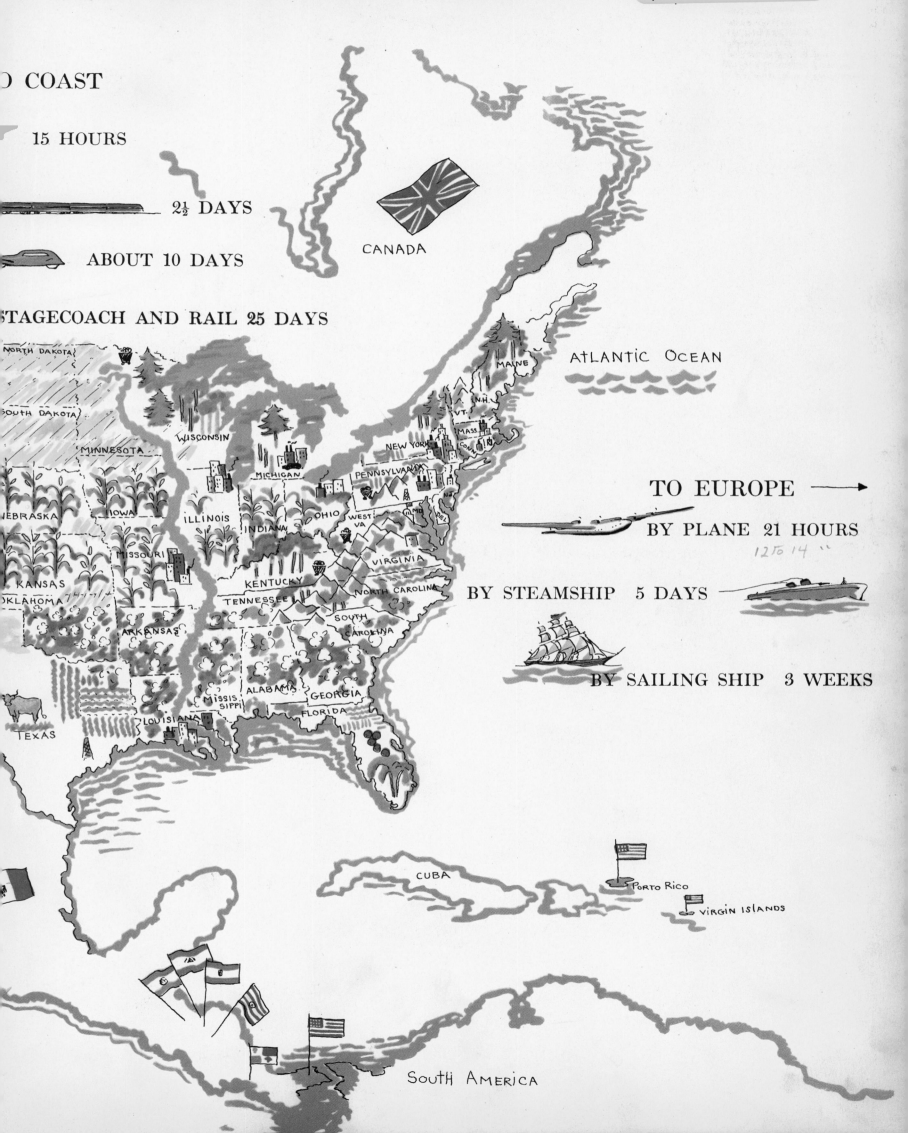

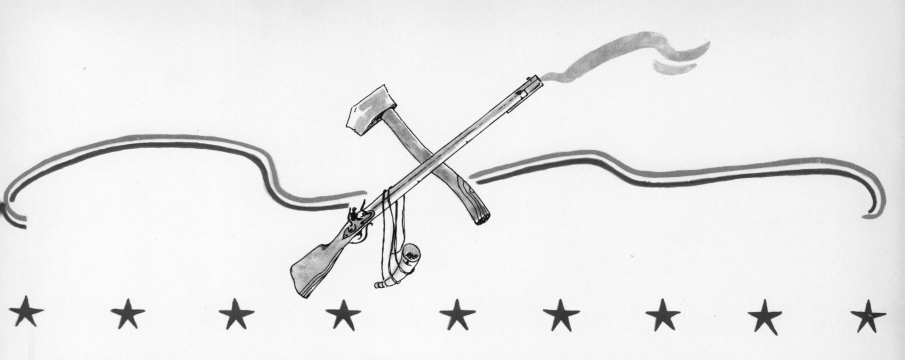

★ ★ ★ ★ ★ ★ ★ ★ ★ ★ ★

THE LITTLE HISTORY

OF

THE UNITED STATES

BY   MABLE   PYNE

ILLUSTRATIONS BY THE AUTHOR

Mable Pyne.

HOUGHTON   MIFFLIN   COMPANY

Boston

For Jennifer Pyne who asks such INT'resting questions.

? ? ? ? ? ? ? ? ? ? ? ? ? ? ? ? ? ? ? ?

Campbell

Ross

CHRISTOPHER COLUMBUS

OCTOBER 12

This really happened about four hundred years ago; before Grandma was a little girl, or her Grandmother, or her Grandma's Grandmother.

Christopher Columbus, a brave man who lived in Italy, was sure he could find a new way to India. India was a land of fine jewels, silks, cotton, pepper and cinnamon.

He went to Spain and begged the King and Queen to help him. Queen Isabella asked some rich men to pay for three ships for him, and they did.

Traders usually went EAST to India. Columbus said he would go WEST and, by going around the world, land on the other side of India. He didn't know that two large oceans and a very large country were in the way.

People laughed or cried when he sailed off with his three small ships, which were about the size of railroad cars. Some said he would fall off the earth; only a fool would think the earth round instead of flat!

Days, weeks, and months went by; no land. Water was getting low, not much food was left. The sailors were frightened; Columbus too, a little. One night they saw light across the water. They could hardly believe it. This meant land . . . at last.

In the morning, they rowed to shore in little boats and were surprised to find reddish-brown men, dressed in a few feathers and skins. Columbus called them Indians because he thought he had reached India.

The Indians were just as surprised to see him. They had never seen people with white skins before. Columbus took some Indians back to Spain with him. He made three more trips across the Atlantic, but always landed on the islands to the south of our country — the West Indies — and once on the coast of South America.

His men were disappointed because they found no jewels nor spices. They found some gold but not as much as they expected. Although Columbus discovered a new world he died a poor man.

This is where Columbus landed, and this is the kind of Indian Columbus expected to find.

PACIFIC

ATLANTIC

BALBOA

OTHER EXPLORERS FOLLOW COLUMBUS' SEA STEPS

From Spain and England, other ships set out. The Spaniards landed down around Mexico and the English landed in Canada; but no one stayed long.

AMERIGO — AMERICA

People began to call this new world America after reading the reports of Amerigo Vespucci who had sailed up and down the South American coast.

In England Sir Walter Raleigh was interested in the new lands. He sent men to explore. The pleasant country they found, he named Virginia.

JAMESTOWN, VIRGINIA

About a hundred years later, in 1607, a boatload of English people landed at Virginia. They had many troubles. Some were sick, others were lazy and the Indians weren't very friendly.

Captain John Smith was one of their leaders. He made the people plant corn and tobacco, and build a fort.

He was once captured by Indians. Just as the Indians were about to kill him, Pocahontas, the Indian Chief's daughter, asked her father to let him go. He did, and the captain went back to his people.

The tobacco sold for a high price in England, so more families came and the large plantations of the South began.

NEW AMSTERDAM

The Half Moon

Then people from Holland came to buy furs from the Indians to send back and sell in Europe. They had heard of this place from Hendrik Hudson who had sailed into the Hudson River several years before, in 1609.

The Dutch landed at New York which had no name then. They called it New Amsterdam, because in Holland there was a city named Amsterdam.

In 1626, Peter Minuit and his settlers gave beads, and hammers, and axes, and bright cloth to the Indians. And the Indians said, 'You may have this island of Manhattan.' What is now New York City cost about twenty-four dollars.

The Indians didn't quarrel with these newcomers. Instead they brought beaver and otter skins to trade for more beads and tools.

Farms were started, houses and windmills like those in Holland were built, and the people were happy.

News of war between Holland and England alarmed the town and they built a wall across the island. It was where Wall Street is now.

King Charles of England said New Amsterdam was his and gave it to his brother the Duke of York.

The Dutch didn't like that very much, but their fort and army were small and when three ships filled with English soldiers came into the harbor, they decided not to fight.

Angry Peter Stuyvesant, the Governor, took down the Dutch flag, put up the English one and the name of the town was changed to New York.

PLYMOUTH ROCK

PLYMOUTH, MASSACHUSETTS

The Pilgrims, who were not allowed to have the kind of church they wanted in England, landed in 1620 on the rocky coast of Massachusetts after a terribly long and stormy trip in the little ship Mayflower.

When the ship sailed back, they must have felt small and lonely. It was fall, and they faced winter in this wilderness.

But the Pilgrims were strong and built cabins of hewn timber, with thatched roofs, fished and hunted for food.

Sometimes the Indians shot arrows at them, and at other times helped them. The Indians showed the white men how to plant and use food they had never seen before — food like corn and potatoes.

The next year, the Pilgrims grew lots of food, and were happy and thankful. They had a feast to which they invited the Indians. This was the first

THANKSGIVING

Each year since then, when the last pumpkin has been brought in from the field, people have had a Thanksgiving feast.

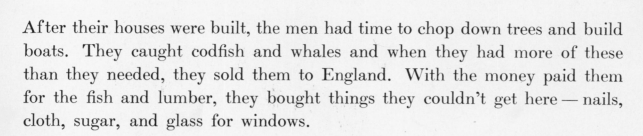

After their houses were built, the men had time to chop down trees and build boats. They caught codfish and whales and when they had more of these than they needed, they sold them to England. With the money paid them for the fish and lumber, they bought things they couldn't get here — nails, cloth, sugar, and glass for windows.

Other people in England heard it was possible to live in America, so they came too. Soon English people lived in Boston and in little towns of Connecticut and Rhode Island. This part of the country came to be known as NEW England.

Lord Baltimore and his Catholic followers settled in Maryland; William Penn and his Quakers, in Pennsylvania.

The women worked every minute, spinning and weaving the wool for clothes, cooking, baking and sewing.

Even candles and soap had to be made at home. The children helped and they were also taught reading and writing. Everyone went to church very often.

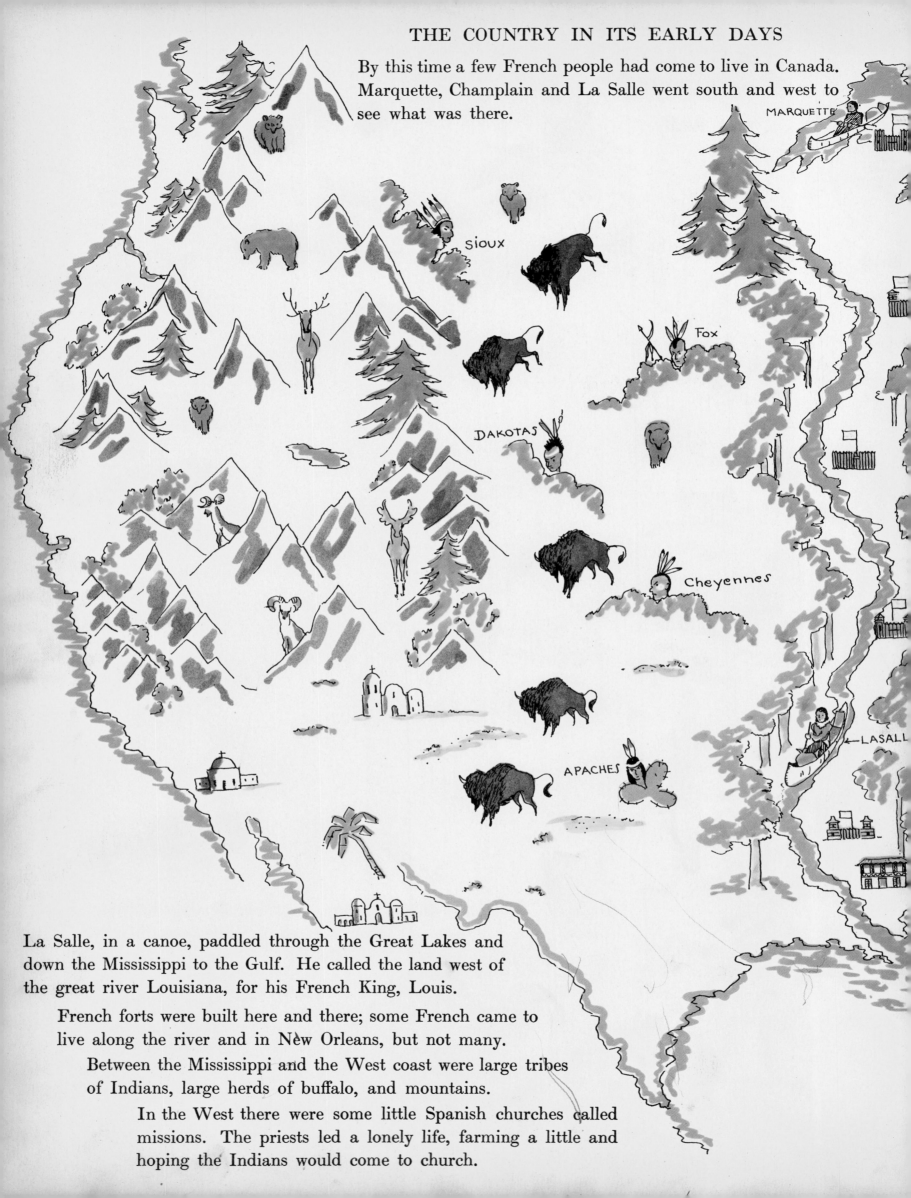

THE COUNTRY IN ITS EARLY DAYS

By this time a few French people had come to live in Canada. Marquette, Champlain and La Salle went south and west to see what was there.

MARQUETTE

SIOUX

FOX

DAKOTAS

Cheyennes

LASALLE

APACHES

La Salle, in a canoe, paddled through the Great Lakes and down the Mississippi to the Gulf. He called the land west of the great river Louisiana, for his French King, Louis.

French forts were built here and there; some French came to live along the river and in New Orleans, but not many.

Between the Mississippi and the West coast were large tribes of Indians, large herds of buffalo, and mountains.

In the West there were some little Spanish churches called missions. The priests led a lonely life, farming a little and hoping the Indians would come to church.

Now there were settlements, all up and down the Atlantic Coast. The Indians had moved west a little.

People in the North sent oil, furs, fish and lumber to Europe.

People in the South sent rice and tobacco and potatoes.

Coming to the new country were ships with families; and, it is sad to say, ships with Negro slaves from Africa to work in the hot fields of the South.

MORE PEOPLE COME

As more and more Germans, Swedes, Irish and English landed, towns grew. Animals and Indians took to the woods westward. Hunters followed.

After the hunters came families. With ax and rifle they made their way into Kentucky. Daniel Boone, who knew the ways and language of the Indians, led them through the Cumberland Gap. They built their houses near a stockade — a square fort made of log fences. These people were called Pioneers. Pioneer means the first one to live in a new and strange land.

In the East, mills were built to grind corn and saw logs. Water turned the wheels which turned big grinding stones and saws inside the mills. This was much easier and faster than doing it by hand. Harvard and Yale colleges were built and about four hundred ships were fishing off the New England coast.

People in the South had sold so much tobacco and cotton that they had plenty of money. They built beautiful homes and ordered fine clothes and furniture from England.

THE REVOLUTION

The people in the American colonies grew tired of having a far-away king tell them what to do, and very tired of having to pay the King money.

England charged them much more for tea than the Dutch did and, what's more, said they HAD to buy it. One night, some white men dressed as Indians, went on board a British ship anchored at Boston and threw boxes of expensive tea into the water. This was called the Boston Tea Party.

The British sent soldiers to keep order, and stopped all ships from coming into the harbor.

The other colonies — each settled section was a colony — sent food and money to the people of Boston. The men of Massachusetts secretly collected muskets and hid them at Concord. These men were ready to leave their homes and fields at any moment, and were called Minute Men.

The British sent out soldiers to take away these guns but Paul Revere rode all night through the country telling the people that the British were coming. The New Englanders were ready in the morning and fought with the British at Lexington and Concord.

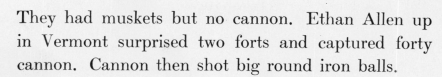

They had muskets but no cannon. Ethan Allen up in Vermont surprised two forts and captured forty cannon. Cannon then shot big round iron balls.

The Colonists had learned from the Indians a way of fighting that the British didn't understand. Instead of marching and fighting in rows, they appeared suddenly from behind rocks and trees.

There was a story that Betsy Ross, a friend of George Washington, sewed the first flag, with 13 stripes and 13 stars — one for each colony.

At a meeting of men from all the colonies, now called States, a paper was written which declared our Independence. That means we wanted to make our own rules and be free from the King and his soldiers. This happened on the 4th of July (Firecracker day) 1776 and all men got their guns ready to help chase the British out of the country. They chose George Washington to lead them.

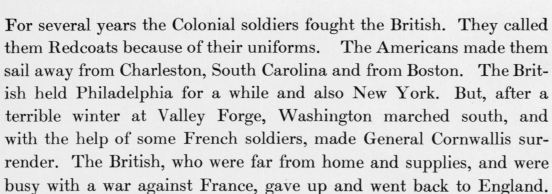

This was the Revolution. Revolution is a quick, sudden change of leaders, laws and living.

For several years the Colonial soldiers fought the British. They called them Redcoats because of their uniforms. The Americans made them sail away from Charleston, South Carolina and from Boston. The British held Philadelphia for a while and also New York. But, after a terrible winter at Valley Forge, Washington marched south, and with the help of some French soldiers, made General Cornwallis surrender. The British, who were far from home and supplies, and were busy with a war against France, gave up and went back to England.

MOUNT VERNON

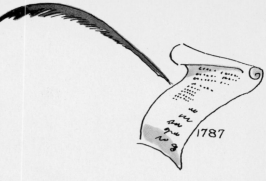

1787

Six years after the fighting had stopped our Constitution was written and signed by a Congress which was a group or committee of men from all the states.

The Constitution is a set of rules about how to manage the country and its people. It also tells us how to elect a President and his helpers. The people elected General Washington for their first President.

We have a holiday on George Washington's birthday, February 22nd.

Benjamin Franklin was a friend of Washington. He is famous for the many things he did. He started the delivery of letters between Philadelphia and New York; a man on horseback took the mail. He printed a newspaper, started a lending library and made the first rocking chair.

With a kite and string and a key he found out that lightning is electricity in the sky.

He went to ask the King of France to help us when we were at war with England.

$15,000,000

THE COUNTRY GROWS

1803

Then we bought Louisiana from France for fifteen million dollars. This was the whole middle section of the United States.

President Thomas Jefferson sent Captain Meriwether Lewis and Captain William Clark to look over this wilderness for him.

They started northwest with two horses, three boats, some soldiers, a few Kentucky riflemen and NO maps. From an Indian village they took along a French-Canadian guide, his Indian wife Sacajawea and their baby. The Indians were useful because they knew some of the Indian tribes and their languages.

CAPTAIN AND CAPTAIN
LEWIS CLARK

It took ONE YEAR to get through the forests. On the way Lewis and Clark had trouble with bears, had to carry canoes and boxes around waterfalls, and couldn't cross the mountains in the winter because of high snowdrifts. They went on to Oregon over in the northwest corner, and finally drifted down the Columbia River to the Pacific. By then their moccasins were worn out.

Portage

Little James Watt had watched the cover of a tea kettle bounce, and thought that if a little steam could do that, a lot of steam could turn wheels. When he grew up he made a steam engine that did turn wheels.

1769

Then Robert Fulton put one of those engines in a boat, the Clermont. The boat went through the water of the Hudson River and didn't need sails or wind. People were amazed.

The Clermont · 1807

Guerrière   Constitution

ANOTHER WAR

With England again, about letting our ships go where they wanted. This was the War of 1812.

We had only a few fighting ships then but our ships had fine sailors and captains. We won the war on sea with the help of a strong ship, the Constitution. Ships were still made of wood but this one was called Old Ironsides because shot seemed to bounce off her.

On land, our soldiers didn't do so well at first. The British chased them from Washington and, after eating a dinner that had been cooked for guests of the President, they set fire to the city. Mrs. Madison, the President's wife, left in a hurry but told a servant to save George Washington's picture — the one you see so much.

The British marched on to Baltimore but couldn't take Fort McHenry. During this battle The Star Spangled Banner, our national song, was written by Francis Scott Key, as he watched from an English prison-ship.

Potomac River

General Andrew Jackson, with a small army of western fighters, went to New Orleans and drove off the enemy. Soon after this a treaty (agreement) was signed with the English who were having plenty of trouble with France.

THE COUNTRY CHANGES
BECAUSE THERE ARE ALWAYS PEOPLE WHO WANT TO SEE
WHAT'S AROUND THE CORNER OR ON THE NEXT PAGE

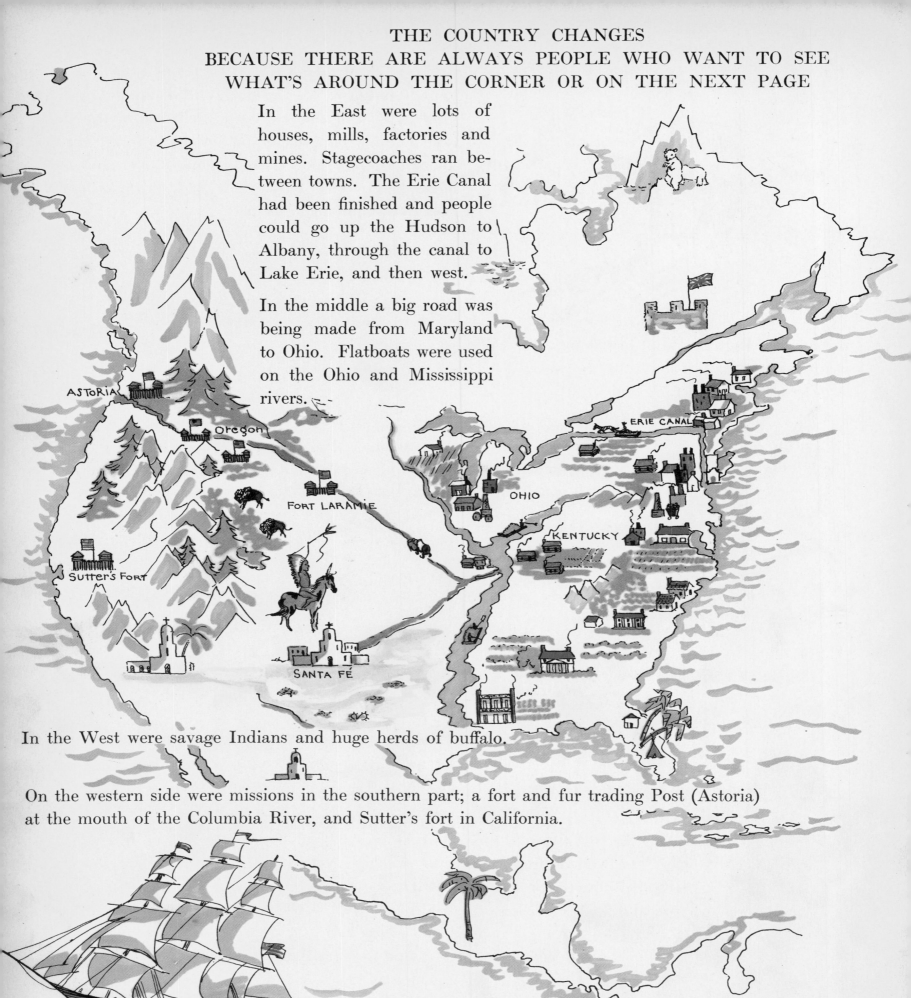

In the East were lots of houses, mills, factories and mines. Stagecoaches ran between towns. The Erie Canal had been finished and people could go up the Hudson to Albany, through the canal to Lake Erie, and then west.

In the middle a big road was being made from Maryland to Ohio. Flatboats were used on the Ohio and Mississippi rivers.

In the West were savage Indians and huge herds of buffalo.

On the western side were missions in the southern part; a fort and fur trading Post (Astoria) at the mouth of the Columbia River, and Sutter's fort in California.

AND
going down around the dangerous tip of South America, were
CLIPPER SHIPS OF NEW ENGLAND
fast, slim ships with tall sails. They sailed around to California with things to sell. It took three months or more. And every year they raced to China for the new crop of tea. The Cutty Sark and the Flying Cloud were very famous ships.

OUT THROUGH THE WEST fur traders had built a few forts. Men who felt crowded in the East packed their families and furniture into big covered wagons pulled by oxen, and set out to follow this long Oregon Trail. It took months over mountains and rivers. Often they had to throw out things to lighten the loads.

Because the Indians didn't like to have the West taken from them, war parties often swooped upon the wagon trains. It was safest to travel in large groups.

Men from churches — called Missionaries — tried to make the Indians feel more kindly toward the white farmers BUT the Indians caught measles from the settlers. They had never had measles, wouldn't stay in bed, and rushed into the river when hot with fever. Many of them died. There were fights, killings and burned cabins.

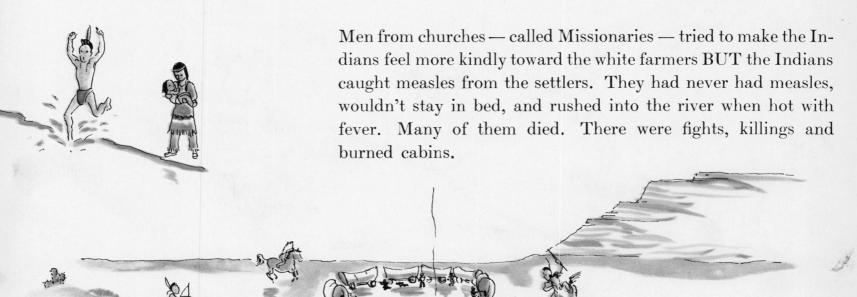

South and West along the trail to Santa Fe men drove wagons loaded, not with settlers, but with goods for sale. The Apache Indians were very savage and when they appeared suddenly the white men had no trees or rocks in this flat country to hide behind. There were also deserts to cross and few people cared to go there.

In Texas the colonists decided to join the other States rather than be part of Mexico. Mexico tried to keep this land. Americans in the Alamo were killed — every one — because they wouldn't give up to a Mexican army ten times their number. Then General Sam Houston came with soldiers from the United States and Santa Anna, the Mexican General, gave up Texas.

Alamo

812   1859

NEW THINGS

1793

1813

People had been using whale oil for lamps, but now oil — petroleum — was found in wells in the ground.

The Cotton-gin, a machine that Eli Whitney made, separated seeds from cotton.

Women stopped spinning and weaving because mills using steam could do it much faster.

On the farms, a reaper could cut more wheat in two hours than six men with scythes could in a whole afternoon.

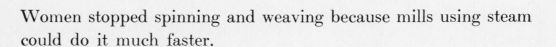

A new kind of gun, the Colt revolver, held six bullets that could be fired one after the other.

SIX-SHOOTER

1844

A man, Samuel Morse, after trying and trying, made a telegraph. It sent signals along wires to a station where a man changed the dots and dashes into words. Telegrams are sent this way.

Andrew Jackson and some soldiers went to Florida to stop the Seminole Indians from making trouble. Then we sent Spain a lot of money to let Florida become part of the United States.

1830

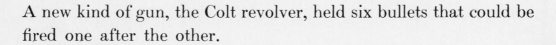

The first little railroad started from Baltimore to Ohio.

Only blacksmiths had been using coal from the mines in Pennsylvania. Wood was getting scarce in the East and people began to use coal in grates and fireplaces.

Men began to use new steel pen nibs instead of the quills from geese.

1858

The Sirius

ACROSS THE ATLANTIC for the first time came steam boats, the Sirius and the Great Western. It took ONLY sixteen days! A great many people came who had been afraid of the long, rough trip on sailing ships. They kept on going west after they landed and began to make the new land into farms.

Women still sewed most of their clothes, but a new machine now helped them by sewing for them. They had no electricity then, but pumping a treadle with the foot made the wheel go around and the needle up and down. Elias Howe thought of it in 1846.

Housewives baked all their bread and 'put up' food and jellies in jars. Water had to be heated in a kettle on the stove, and washstands were in every bedroom. The houses had no bathrooms! To wash, you had to pour water from a pitcher into the china basin and empty the soapy water into a big jar. It took so long to heat enough water for a bath that people took one only about once a week. That's why people joke about Saturday night; a day for washing, a day for ironing, and a day for bathing.

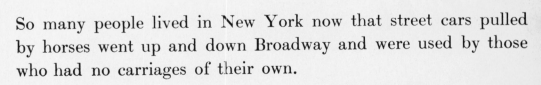

So many people lived in New York now that street cars pulled by horses went up and down Broadway and were used by those who had no carriages of their own.

GOLD — WHERE? — THE RUSH TO CALIFORNIA

At Sutter's fort, while men were building a sawmill, they found flakes of gold in the water.

Everywhere men dropped their work, left ships and families. Roads to the West were crowded. Freight wagons took supplies for the new tent cities, but this was too slow for the mail and gold. So a stagecoach line was started. The driver sat on a high seat, not only to manage his six horses, but to watch for Indians and robbers.

Still faster — for mail — was the Pony Express from St. Joseph, Missouri to California. It was like a relay race. At stations along the way, the rider changed from his tired pony to a fresh one which was saddled and waiting for him. If the station had been burned by Indians, as sometimes happened, he had to ride on to the next station.

Then, faster than any of these, when the poles and wires had been strung across the country, went messages by telegraph.

THE WAR BETWEEN THE STATES

The people of the North and the people of the South couldn't agree about a number of things; one of which was slavery. There were now a great many Negroes in the south. Their owners usually took good care of them.

But the North and South argued, and the Southern States finally said they'd leave the Union and have their own President and flag.

Abraham Lincoln was President and wanted to keep the country together. When the Southerners took Fort Sumter, a United States fort in South Carolina, he sent soldiers and the War between the States began.

The South surprised the North by sinking two wooden ships with their battleship, the Merrimac. It had iron plates on its sides. Next day, down from the North came the Monitor, iron clad too, with guns shooting from a turret that could turn.

ABRAHAM LINCOLN — FEBRUARY 12

General Ulysses S. Grant, leading the soldiers of the North, called Federals, marched south against General Robert E. Lee and his Confederates.

Part of Grant's army fought their way down the Mississippi River and General Sherman marched across the South to Georgia; taking cattle and corn and horses and destroying property on the way.

Northern ships anchored off the southern ports and kept food and guns from being brought in. Although the Southern soldiers fought bravely, they had to surrender.

There had been terrible battles like the one at Gettysburg which lasted three days, and everyone was glad when the war ended. The Southern plantations were split up, and the South grew vegetables as well as cotton, and built factories for spinning.

Ever since then, colored people have been free to work where, and for what they want.

We celebrate Abraham Lincoln's birthday, February 12th, because he was a kind and good president.

A crazy actor shot him at a theatre in Washington soon after the war ended.

THE INDIAN LOSES

SAN FRANCISCO   NEW YORK

Close to the Oregon Trail the Union Pacific Company built a railroad across the country. It took seven days and seven nights to go from New York to California and the Pullmans had candle-light, and small stoves at both ends of the cars.

The Indians made a last desperate attempt to keep the white man out of what was left of their hunting grounds. Tribes joined together and attacked the settlers and railroad builders.

Soldiers were sent out to force them to stay in certain places, called Reservations. Small groups of soldiers had to fight Indian war parties of thousands.

General Custer and his cavalry were all killed by a band of Sioux, led by Sitting Bull.

Buffalo Bill Cody, who had been a Pony Express rider, helped the soldiers, and kept the Cheyennes from joining the Sioux. He shot their chief, Yellow Hand.

CUSTER

INDIAN RESERVATION

It took a long time to make the Apaches stop their raids. They had kept Arizona and New Mexico in terror. At last the railroad to Santa Fe could be finished.

THE WILD WEST

Now the cowboy appeared on the plains with his cattle. He followed the trails the buffalo had used; when the grass dried up, he drove his herds from Texas north to Montana.

This was called the Long Drive and it WAS long — so long and lonesome that when they reached a town, the cowboys were ready to celebrate.

They shot off their guns for fun, they danced and drank, spent money, and had fights. Some men wore two guns! The sheriffs had such a hard time trying to keep order and stop the many train robberies, that this part of the country became known as the Wild West

AND

In Chicago, a woman's cow kicked over a lantern — so the story goes — and almost all of the large city burned.

1871

Alaska, that jutting-out piece of land above Canada, was bought from Russia.

A cable — a big wire with smaller wires inside it — was laid across the bottom of the Atlantic Ocean between Europe and America. Telegrams could be sent through this cable which meant no more long waits for news.

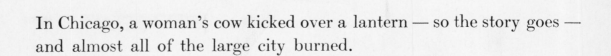

Streets in New York were crowded with horsedrawn trucks and carriages. An elevated train was built which ran on tracks above the street.

Many people, young and old, rode on bicycles. Perhaps your Grandma and Grandpa used to ride on a tandem. It had two seats and two sets of pedals.

Into business offices came a new machine, the typewriter, for writing letters quickly.

The very first phonograph was made. It was a surprise to hear voices or music come out of a horn.

A few people had gas lights and gas stoves. It was pleasant, in hot weather, not to have to cook on a hot coal stove.

People laughed at a strange carriage that went without a horse to pull it. 'Get a horse,' they yelled, when something went wrong with it, which was pretty often. Some people were cross because it frightened their horses. This first automobile had to be wound up by hand to make it start. It went slowly, moving in a cloud of dust because, except in cities, all the roads were of dirt.

For the first time, mothers could buy soup in a can, instead of cooking it in a pot all day long.

In the West people used the new barbed wire for fences: cattle were kept on farms and 'long drives' were over.

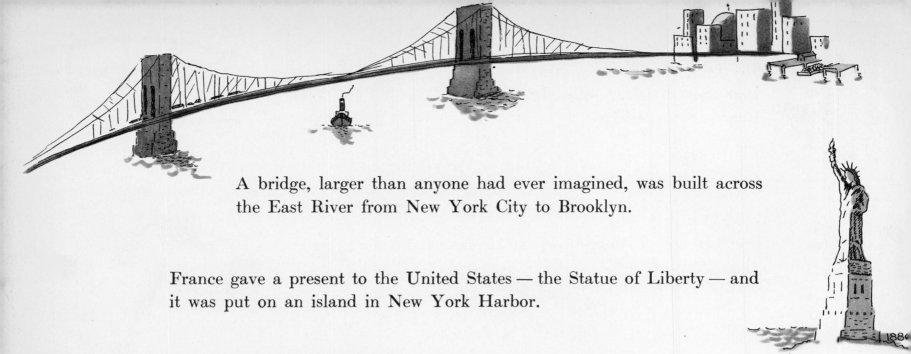

A bridge, larger than anyone had ever imagined, was built across the East River from New York City to Brooklyn.

France gave a present to the United States — the Statue of Liberty — and it was put on an island in New York Harbor.

Alexander Graham Bell's telephone began to be used.

1876

Machines could do more and more. One, a harvester, not only cut the wheat, but cleaned it and put it in bags.

Fire engines had a little fire in them to make steam pump the water through the hose. They were called 'Steamers.' Each Engine company had a 'Fire' Dog, always white with black spots, that ran beside the horses to every fire.

The Maine, one of our battleships, while anchored near the Spanish island of Cuba, was blown up. We had a short war with Spain about it.

1898

With the United States soldiers who landed in Cuba, was Theodore Roosevelt — later our President — and his Rough Riders. After we won a battle at San Juan Hill and sank the Spanish fleets at Santiago and the Philippine Islands, Spain asked for peace and gave these islands to us.

In the early 1900's everyone was talking about pictures that moved. They were short and 'silent': that is, there was no sound effect.

1903

On land and at sea began the use of a telegraph that sent messages through the air. No wires were needed. It was called Wireless.

And two brothers named Wright made an airplane that could fly with a man in it. People could hardly believe it.

1903

A store and a few homes put in a new kind of light. You could turn a button and a bright light shone in the glass globe. Thomas Edison, who invented it, was called a 'Wizard.'

Enormous furnaces made plenty of steel for trains and buildings and boats and cars. More things than people here needed came from the mills and factories and were sold to other countries. That made the country rich. That means most of the people here had enough money to live more comfortably than did the working people of other countries.

Hawaii became part of the United States.

1900

The Panama Canal was built after a war on mosquitoes. Panama had sold us a 10 mile wide strip of land from ocean to ocean. Yellow fever had kept other people from digging a canal. The United States sent Walter Reed, a doctor, who found that mosquitoes carried the germs. Colonel Gorgas cleaned up the swamps from which they came. The canal saves ships an 8000 mile trip around South America.

Gold was found in Alaska and the miners who rushed there were glad we had bought the country.

THEN IN 1914

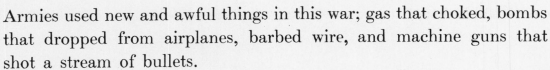

A big fight started across the ocean in Europe. It was called the World War because almost every country in the world pitched in.

The United States didn't join it until too many of her ships were sunk by the new German submarines. We sent soldiers, guns and food, in charge of General John J. Pershing.

Armies used new and awful things in this war; gas that choked, bombs that dropped from airplanes, barbed wire, and machine guns that shot a stream of bullets.

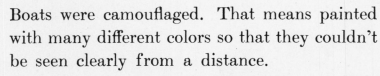

Boats were camouflaged. That means painted with many different colors so that they couldn't be seen clearly from a distance.

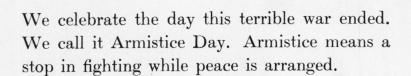

We celebrate the day this terrible war ended. We call it Armistice Day. Armistice means a stop in fighting while peace is arranged.

Schools closed, everyone marched. Whistles blew. Everyone was happy because the soldiers would come home.

ARMISTICE DAY — NOVEMBER 11th.

Radio broadcasts began. You had to have earphones — something like earmuffs — to hear the programs. They were connected by a wire to the radio set.

Lots of families bought cars which were closed in and started without cranking. Telephones were put in many houses.

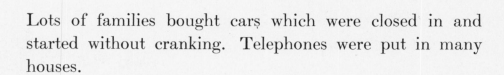

Airplanes started to carry mail.

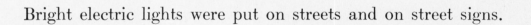

In 1927 Charles A. Lindbergh flew alone in a small airplane across the Atlantic Ocean right to Paris where he had planned to go. He left in the morning, flew all day and all that night and landed late the next afternoon, very sleepy.

Women had ALWAYS had long hair, but quite suddenly hundreds, then thousands, cut their hair short and their skirts too. They could vote at last. Until now they hadn't been allowed to help choose the President.

Bright electric lights were put on streets and on street signs.

And motion pictures began to talk. At first they only made sounds — like whistling for trains — and then, strange grumbling voices. But men worked and worked to make them better. So many people went to the 'movies' that we had to have huge theaters to take care of them.

Boats were built larger and went faster. Because there was no more room for new buildings, New York made its buildings higher. They were called skyscrapers because it seemed as if their tops must scrape against the sky.

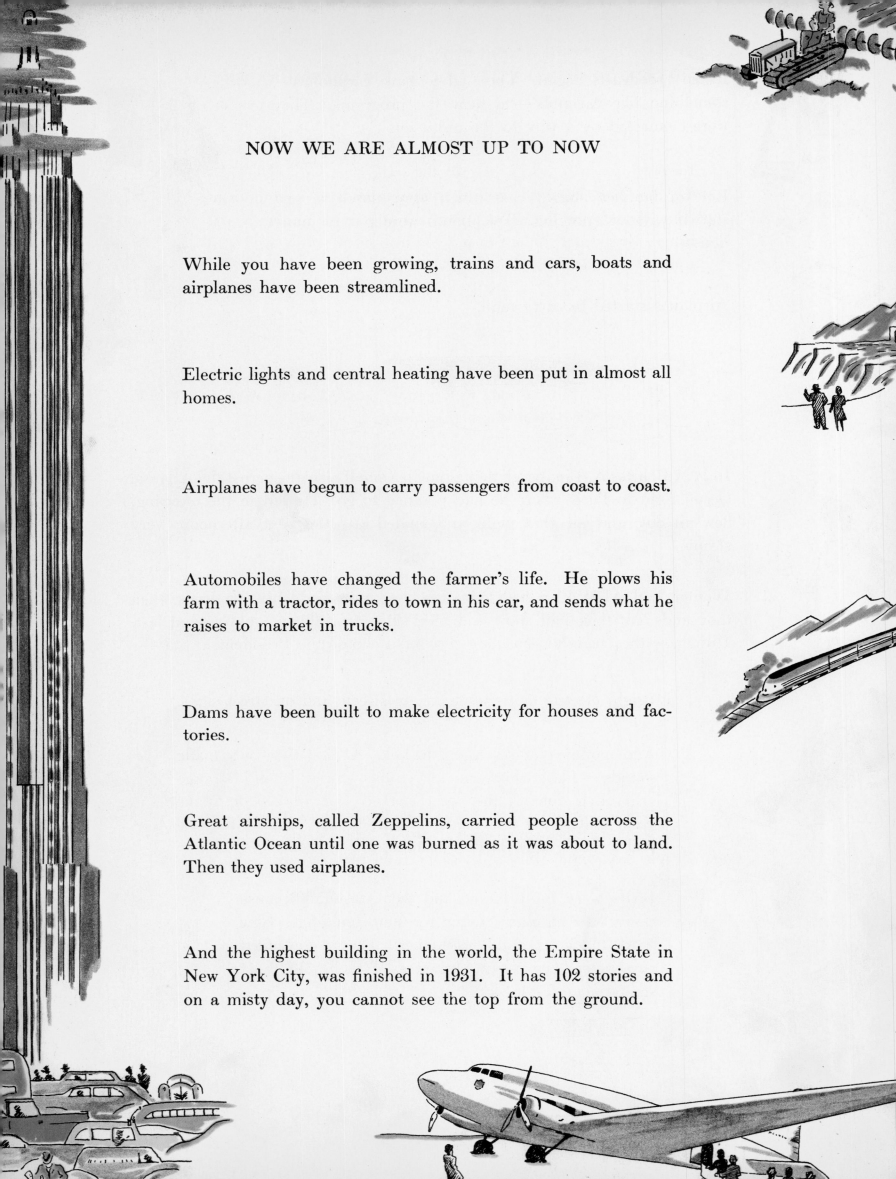

NOW WE ARE ALMOST UP TO NOW

While you have been growing, trains and cars, boats and airplanes have been streamlined.

Electric lights and central heating have been put in almost all homes.

Airplanes have begun to carry passengers from coast to coast.

Automobiles have changed the farmer's life. He plows his farm with a tractor, rides to town in his car, and sends what he raises to market in trucks.

Dams have been built to make electricity for houses and factories.

Great airships, called Zeppelins, carried people across the Atlantic Ocean until one was burned as it was about to land. Then they used airplanes.

And the highest building in the world, the Empire State in New York City, was finished in 1931. It has 102 stories and on a misty day, you cannot see the top from the ground.

WORK AROUND THE HOUSE BECOMES EASIER

By putting a wire into a plug in the wall, electricity makes the ice, the toast, runs the washing machine and the vacuum machine that cleans the house. It mixes and cooks, and sews and irons. Grandmother had to put her iron on the stove and wait until it became hot.

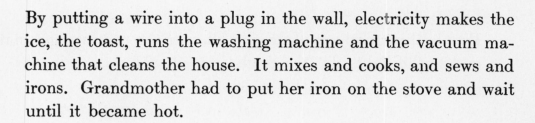

Fast refrigerated trains bring fresh fruits and vegetables from far-off farms. Not so long ago, people couldn't have oranges unless they lived near where they grew.

Nearly every kind of food is canned; even gravy!

Women have more time because housework doesn't take so long. Many girls, because there is no need to help their mothers, go to work. Some mothers, too. People have more time to go places and play out of doors.

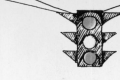

NOW

People think nothing of driving all over the country; gas stations and traffic lights dot the roads instead of forts.

Big airplanes, the Clippers, carry mail and passengers across the Pacific to China and across the Atlantic to Europe.

Machines do almost everything; sort fruit, dig tunnels, make bread, raise bridges, and milk cows.

In Washington, you can see broad streets lined with beautiful government buildings, and thousands of workers helping to run the government;—and perhaps you can see the President.

In California, you can cross two of the most wonderful bridges in the world. You can see a town grown large because motion pictures are made there; and you can see fruits and vegetables growing for the markets all over the country.

In the Middle West, you can see hundreds of automobiles coming out of the factories of Michigan; and corn and cattle coming into Chicago, that city between the East and West.

In Florida you can see people arriving from all over, when winter roars across the country.

NOW AND TOMORROW

What happens next, you'll see and read about.
While you grow, your country and the things about you grow and change.
What happens now becomes history later.

Presidents and other leaders talk to you on the radio and, when engineers finish their work on television, you may be able to see, as well as hear them.

You can go to the top of the highest building in the world.

You can go into restaurants and movies on a roasting hot day and find the air cooled for you.

You can ice-skate outdoors, even though the day is rather warm. A machine makes the ice.

You can ride in an elevator that goes and stops when you push a button.

And as you grow older you'll probably see many more wonderful things happen; because, in this country, people have always looked for new and better ways of doing and making things; newer and better ways of living.

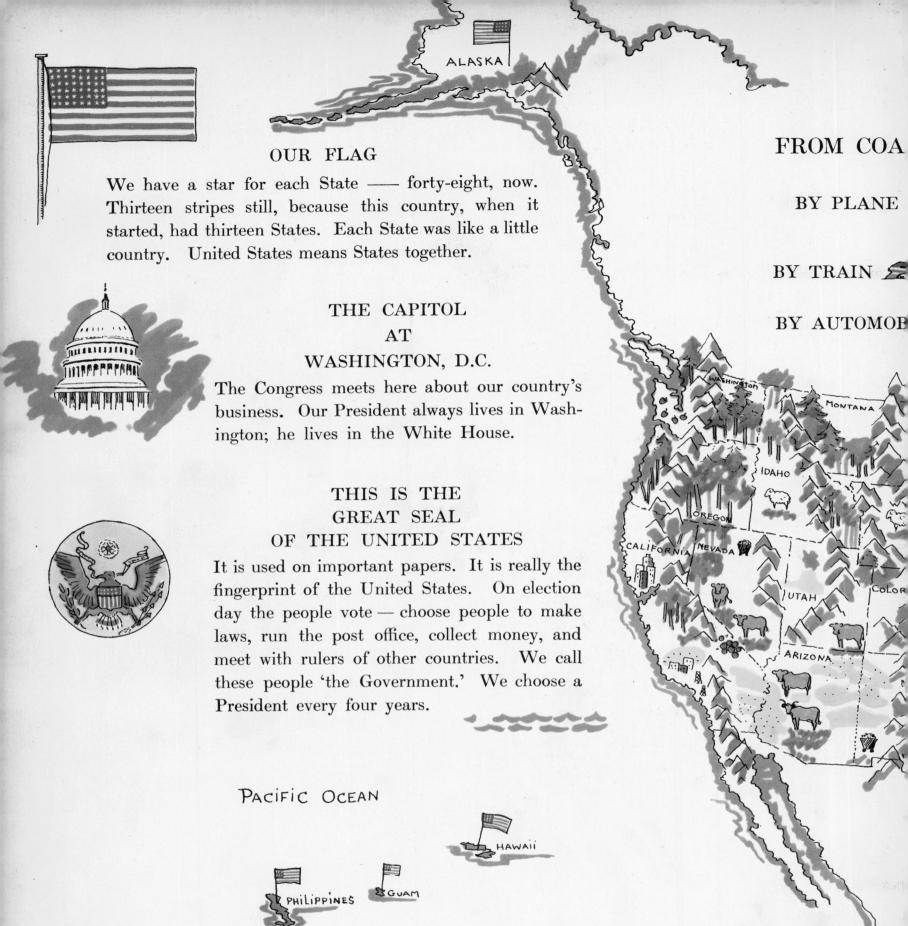

OUR FLAG

We have a star for each State —— forty-eight, now. Thirteen stripes still, because this country, when it started, had thirteen States. Each State was like a little country. United States means States together.

THE CAPITOL
AT
WASHINGTON, D.C.

The Congress meets here about our country's business. Our President always lives in Washington; he lives in the White House.

THIS IS THE
GREAT SEAL
OF THE UNITED STATES

It is used on important papers. It is really the fingerprint of the United States. On election day the people vote — choose people to make laws, run the post office, collect money, and meet with rulers of other countries. We call these people 'the Governmint.' We choose a President every four years.

PACIFIC OCEAN

HAWAII

PHILIPPINES   GUAM

FROM COA

BY PLANE

BY TRAIN

BY AUTOMOB

ALASKA

WASHINGTON   MONTANA

IDAHO

OREGON

CALIFORNIA   NEVADA

UTAH   COLOR

ARIZONA

⟵ TO CHINA

BY PLANE   6 DAYS

BY STEAMSHIP   19 DAYS

BY SAILING SHIP   35 DAYS